BITTER-SWEET

Ross A. Henderson

ARTHUR H. STOCKWELL LTD
Torrs Park   Ilfracombe   Devon
Established 1898
www.ahstockwell.co.uk

British Library Cataloguing-in-Publication Data.
A catalogue record for this book is available
from the British Library.

CIAC
DONATION 7/5
K 2734951003
821.92 HEN

ISBN 978-0-7223-4103-2
Printed in Great Britain by
Arthur H. Stockwell Ltd
Torrs Park   Ilfracombe
Devon

CONTENTS

SUBTERRANEAN EXPLOSION

Subterranean explosion,
Break-out tips emerge,
Spring's green silent surge
Confirming true resurrection.

Sun-seeking tubers,
Space-squeezing creepers,
Branch-bowing leafers,
Bud-bursting fruiters.

Feed me the formula:
Sap-stinging stamina
And mind-spurting semen.
I am the superman.

COOL LIKE A DARK POOL

Cool
Like a dark pool

Lean
Like a skull's mien

Hard
Like a way barred

Strong
Like a steel thong

Quick
Like a pin's prick

Gone
Like today's dawn.

STALACTITIC

Stalactitic
Patiently piercing heartsick walls.
Prick and poke,
Prick and poke,
Wheedling, needling,
Love runs red.

Parasitic
Stealthily stifling heartache calls.
Stick and choke,
Stick and choke,
Feeding, breeding,
Love has fled.

Monolithic
Cruelly crowding heartbreak falls.
Kick and joke,
Kick and joke,
Cheering, jeering,
Love is dead.

ANOTHER WET SUNDAY

Another wet Sunday:
Sodden slouching trees,
Birds bedraggled and forlorn
On the rain-browned fence.

Leaves and things and plastic wrappers
Jostle down the sputtering gutters.
Chameleon pools lurk smooth and still,
The walker's careless feet to chill.

Inside a restless lethargy,
Crumbs and coffee mugs half empty
The *Mail on Sunday* strewn about,
Local radio braying out.

Renewal bleeps Monday
Mobile hustling pleas
In buzzing ether borne
Clamouring for sense.

THE BIRD BATH IS BEREFT

The bird bath is bereft
Because you left.
The garden seat's forlorn
Because you're gone.
The hanging basket's done –
Your time is run.

We are distraught.
So hard you fought.
All cast adrift –
Lost love your gift.

DARKNESS GENTLY LAPS

Darkness gently laps
The edge of day,
Round jagg'd outcrops wraps
Its balmy way.

He rides the black dolphin
Through the deep dark serene,
Down chasms of mystery,
Past tangles of tertiary
In uncharted motion
Where dreams gleam and glisten.

New light lunges
Through night's high reaches,
Tumbles and plunges
Down to dawn's beaches.

SOLID, ROUGHCAST

Solid, roughcast,
Weathered in time;
Heart beats of age,
Vibrations of span.

Disturbed perspectives,
Alignments offset,
Indistinct margins,
Beyond, behind linked.

Myriad particles,
Irruptions in light,
Ions of conscience,
Enigmas of dust.

A THICK SQUALL

A thick squall of gulls screaming,
Careening in mock-making war
Round the red-bowed boat beating
Toward the stilt-armed harbour wall.

Rush of rollers slow-toppling
Fingering dense supine stretches,
Riffling flocks of webbed squabbling
Logged in the stick-legged dawn watches.

Far-off pincushion figures
Twitching in the web of distance,
Tough winds fresh from bleak vigils
Bristling with stiff-ribbed defiance.

Imprints of a sharp-tongued tide
Beyond the woven walls of time.

UNDER THE PINE TREE

Under the pine tree there he sat –
Book, beer and panama hat –
At ease with his time and place
After the honest hard-run race.

Now I rest in dappled shade
Under the pine tree where he's laid.

BITTER-SWEET

Bitter-sweet
Was just a word
Till I saw her
In the street.

Short blonde hair,
Boyish figure,
Jeans and jumper –
Unaware.

She walks free round the corner;
Traffic goes, takes me from her.
The past's umbilical cord
Draws tight and pulls me toward
That time when youth's brash vigour
Brooked no false inhibitor.

And what of her? If she knew,
Would old passions flare anew?
Life goes on and blurs the dream;
Time and people push in between.
Suddenly out bursts the flame,
Bright and sharp and edged with pain.

Short blonde hair,
Boyish figure,
Jeans and jumper –
Unaware.

Bitter-sweet
Was just a word
Till I saw her
In the street.

PINPRICKS OF LIFE

Pinpricks of life
Shimmer
In the distance,
Pulsing.

Flashpoints of strife
Zoom in
Out of focus,
Passing.

Snapshots of love
Burn white
From the inside,
Branding.

Black-and-white frames
Swirl round
In time's mixer,
Blending.

SPIDER WEAVES

Spider weaves,
Old man peeves,
Rose beguiles,
Mother smiles.

Tick-tock,
Hot rock.

Dolphin rolls,
Friend consoles,
Moonlight beams,
Lover dreams.

Sun clock
Stopcock.

Swallow flicks,
Baby kicks,
Heaven spins,
Devil grins.

Time lock
Ice block.

BEDLAM BOUNDS

Bedlam bounds through jaded portal,
Cascades carefree down the hill,
Whirls around the rank and file –
Wary, watchful, quick to rile –
A caravan of life's recruits
Rendezvousing just past Boots
Where stands their chosen casbah.
Legend notes: 'The Castle Snack Bar'.

'Private. No Entry.
Four to five thirty.'

Girls
Grouped in a corner,
Giggling, averting,
Yet womanly sly.
Boys
Boxed in the centre,
Basking, diverting,
Half catching their eye.

Seeking connection,
Fearing rejection.

"Klang!" the silent klaxon goes.
Cokes are downed and chit-chat slows,
Scrape of chair,
Flick of hair –
Exodus.
To catch the bus
Home to 'question time' and tea
And other people's reality.

In London, Montreal, Hong Kong,
Whilst mingling with the midday throng
Is startled by a random vision
Of Castle Street in private session,
And baulks as memories run rife –
A boulder in the stream of life.

For some the journey is complete;
The rest are still out on the beat.

FOREIGN THIS LAND

Foreign this land,
Guzzling man's land.

Secret, dark, cloaked,
Blind faith invoked.

Each day the same,
This razored game.

Maybe today
A foot astray.

Lost in the sand
In the wasteland.

By someone's hand,
Someone's command.

Written in red,
Soldier is dead.

BRASSY GONG

Brassy gong
New-lustred
Beats the dawn
Star-dusted.

Blade carpet
Green-filtered
Stabs upright
Dew-gilted.

Veined digits
Rain-vented
Pipe liquids
Contempered.

Coloured bells
Hue-coded
Light the hills
Splash-coated.

Life circuits
Imprinted
Drive cell chips
Encrypted.